PRAISE FOR

O C E A N

"*O C E A N* is a poetry collection about tides of grief, waves of healing, and the pull of something bigger than the human soul."

   - D. Donovan, Senior Reviewer, *Midwest Book Review*

"*O C E A N* is one of the most unique poetry collections I've ever read. The vivid imagery Lindsey is able to conjure offers an incredible reading experience, only heightened by the absolute raw emotions she infuses."

   - Lindsay Crandall, *Independent Book Review*

"Lindsey's words are not only transformative but they offer a chance to grow and heal. *O C E A N* is a thought-provoking and emotionally resonant collection of poetry that I highly recommend."

   - *Literary Titan*, 5 stars

"A poetry collection that uses spiritual ideas to explore the depths of depression, the transcendent quality of love, and other topics... A heartwarming and affirming set of works."

   - *Kirkus Reviews*

"Lindsey delves into physical and interior landscapes of the human psyche to explore the true nature of love in her poignant debut... Readers will revel in this collection at once reflective and poignant."

   - *BookView Review*, 5 stars

POETRY

ANASTASIA LINDSEY

atmosphere press

I hope these poems find you when you need them the most. You are supported by me, wherever you might be in the world.

With lots of love,

Anastasia.

For My Beautiful Mother Amanda – thank you for everything! From the bottom of my heart, I appreciate you more than I can put into words. All the sacrifices never go unnoticed. Because of you, I am free to chase my dreams. I love you.

Dakota – thank you for being my best friend and partner. Thank you for showing me how to love life again and bringing me safely back to shore. Thank you for seeing me completely and entirely. I love you.

DEEP WATERS

promise me you will not take your life

and leave me here behind

I should have said, all along

that it was you and always will be

I see you hurting, and crying in the shower

I muster up a thought

but always shy away

and baby, I am so sorry for not taking you into my arms

I want to be the man that holds you

one that never hurts you

I see you smile with friends

and I start to hurt inside because I see the tear you wish to shed

you hide it so well for everyone else

but baby, I see you

I want to hug you from behind

and whisper into your ear

'you're safe with me and in my arms, you're protected'

but I stand in the corner like a coward

being a man, my mother did not raise me to be

I have failed you and I am sorry

but promise me you will not take your life

I don't think I will make it without you

I vow to show you my heart

and to hold you when you're down

you're my everlasting love

and from this day on, I promise to be yours too

I dreaded the rain
every time the clouds
came rolling in
I knew it was my collection
of tears from the week
ready to let me have a
taste of my own sadness
the salt burned my eyes
and saturated my skin
it invaded my tastebuds
and left a sour note in my mouth

as a poet, I sometimes forget how to speak

like the words are tangled in my mind

      and on my tongue

I have the words and here they are

but…

they are dressed in stringy lace

and knots are created – like the one currently in my throat

I'm trying to speak

      spoken word

for ears to hear, not just for eyes to see

but I fall back into my comfort zone

      using pen and paper

black scribbled lines connect and flow so easily

like they have rehearsed this many times

when I look into the mirror – I see someone I am disappointed in

her life seems to be falling apart

puffy dark bags under her eyes

grungy clothes and yesterday's makeup – smeared

I see the person I always tried not to be

sad – afraid – alone

I see a woman who has cried herself to sleep

an oversized t-shirt, damp from the tears

I want to ask her how she got here

to this –

a woman with crippled fingers

wanting to dial her lost lovers phone number

I see a flower that has lost all its petals

a wonderer on rigid seas

soul searching

I lie in darkness, as the light slips under the crack of the door

I did it to myself

the light crept out with every negative thought about myself

it tip toed silently to avoid waking me

to avoid the cracking noise of the hardwood floors

I was awake for it all; I saw the light leave

and my body went cold

limp on the hardwood floor, my cheek pressed against the deep

mahogany

I can see the light lingering outside of the door

and I softly lift my fingers to wave goodbye

I sing a lullaby

'bye-bye fireflies'

'so long shooting stars'

'farewell moonlight beams'

I close my eyelids

I'm falling asleep…. 'goodnight, nightlight'

we were so back and forth

so off and on —

I knew the moment you came back

you would be leaving again

so, I stopped getting sad and depressed

instead — I held the door wide open

for the next time you'd leave again

If tomorrow starts without me

and you tear the bed apart, searching for pieces of me

as tears are falling from your face and with an over beating heart

know that I am closer than you think

I am the branch that blows in the wind

right outside of our bedroom window

I am the bird that lands

on the tree of our carved initials

when you step outside

and begin cursing the ground

I am the wind that sweeps across your face

I am the first star in the sky

that begins to shine

that's me

I am the sun that peaks through the trees with fallen leaves

I whisper into your ear as you lie your head for sleep

that I'm sorry for leaving you at night to weep

I may have left life, but returned as much more

I may have left life, but I did not leave you

drowning in my silence

trying not to lose it

awaiting the sound of the sirens

my heart is broken

and laying outside of my chest

I may not make it through this …

will help come in time?

my favorite sad song

playing in the background

I wonder if the medical responders

have ever brought a broken heart

back to life

in a pool of my own blood, I write the lyrics to 'our song'

I hum to the tune in my head … it's keeping me alive.

your eyes are scanning this poem

you've come with a cluttered mind

you're tired, hurt, and backed into a corner

your chest is heavy

and it's hard to breathe, tired of being fought

instead of fought for

the light within you is dim

as the darkness surrounds you even more,

you sit, anxiously awaiting their call

to feel like you're important, that they care

sadness and your struggling smile have become best friends

you ask for permission to simply exist

you love blindly, knowing betrayal is the neighbor

deep inside, you feel empty and you're waiting to be filled

the ground beneath you is crumbling, bringing you to your knees

I know, I've been there

I have this cage inside of my mind
a place where I have locked myself away
sometimes I go there when I am sad
or when I feel unloved
and in this cage, are filing cabinets
labeled from a-z
stored in the folders are things I hate about myself or my life

  a- annoying, atrocious, awful

  b- big, boring, broken

  c- cold, chaotic, clumsy

  d- damaged, depressed, dreary

the list really does go on –
but I sat in this cage for days on end
I wouldn't speak, smile, or laugh
but how could I, sitting in a place like that?
it's dangerous here
so, you will see on the entrance of the cage
it says "no trespassing"

I can't help but think

that when it rains,

the sky is spilling my secrets

I cry and share my pain

I would whisper to the clouds

the things I never told a soul

my secrets must have been heavy to carry

because —

it's sure raining down on me

weight on my shoulders

hoping you don't let distance separate us

to me, miles mean nothing

and when I feel invisible

I wish you could see me, behind this cloak

my life, it has been traumatic

between breakups and childhood memories

I tend to get scared

like the world is out for me

oh, how cursed I feel to have such a good heart

I need held

tightly

the world is out there

collecting tears like mine

preying on girls who cry themselves to sleep

the weak and the sensitive

I'm not up for war, but I'd fight for us

I show love, tell love, speak love, and embody love

just begging for you to mimic my actions

have you felt pain that kept you up all night?

have you ever begged a lover to love you in return?

have you ever held your chest in pain?

wishing, dreaming, and begging for it to subside

I poured out love and watched it overflow

2am – the tub is filling with water

fuck rose petals for self-love

I'm heartbroken

I submerge into the water

and I start to pray for us

grieving and begging for peace and quiet

to find my peace of mind

I watched you drink down your sorrows

and chase them with liquor

lost all your self-control and direction of us

all those times I mumbled under my breath

'no more second chances'

I mean it, I can't chance it – grieving the loss of myself

I don't need you, and that's a hard pill to swallow

my hands are gripping the steering wheel

and the tears are rolling down my face

because I think of the time that I cannot get back

I'm leaving behind everything that we built

but that shit had a rocky foundation since the beginning

I patched it with blood, sweat, and tears

what great bondage right?

you'd clean it up before visitors arrived

I felt like we were always against each other

me vs. you in this battle

I lost my heart to you

you've shipped it away in a box labeled fragile

who do you call when you can't sleep at night?
where do you go when that cheap apartment
starts to feel lonely?
what do you think when you see yourself in the mirror?
are you ashamed of giving into your temptations?

I remember the nights you shared
how you felt broken like the streetlight outside your bedroom
window
are you still dreaming of me?
and screaming forgiveness through night terrors?
I left and it made you want me more
are you stuck, waiting for me to walk through the door?

I wanted you – but you couldn't see that

every bone in my body would've broken on command

if it meant keeping you

you see, the world doesn't keep spinning

because when you suddenly left

everything around me froze

how does it feel, to be the holder of my pain?

of my grief and my sorrow?

how does it feel to hold a gun in your hands?

pulling the trigger to my emotional heartbreak wounds

all it took was seeing your back facing my heart

when you left and abandoned me

how does it feel to load that gun

and whisper words of goodbye that will pierce my severed lungs?

Are you living peacefully, my painful bullet?

It was quick, some like to say

out of nowhere

I had this dream about the life I wanted to share

… with you

I admit, I was guarded and didn't let you in

I was afraid to lose, I think you were afraid to win

I never said how I was feeling, now it's too late

I thought I was special, and worth the wait

the first thing I asked, 'was it me, or something I did?'

jar of tears fell down my face, I was unable to close that lid

I'm perfect and worthy, don't you know it?

burning so bright for you, like a candle lit

you were fuel, and sprinkled my fire deep inside

and damn I couldn't tell you, instead I went to hide

I could scream, and shout, and fill up our space

but would you see me, staring at your face?

It's easy to say that I wasn't enough, but I know I'm more

I'll pick myself up, and wipe the tears from the floor

I'll be somebody, that star on your television screen

fans and family, you could have been there in-between

I'm lighting this cigarette, watching the smoke rise,

I'd be lying if I said I didn't miss looking into your eyes

I'll say just one more thing

because who knows

what the future will bring

when you think of me, say something out loud,

I'll be listening

leaving you was the hardest thing I had ever done

and not that I expected it

but you never offered me peace

you broke my heart in so many ways

I accepted your mediocre love

because I thought that's all I was worth

I lifted you up when I was low down

gave you my best

I received your worst

put myself to the side

to give you all the light

I told you my fears

and you watched them consume me

I remember my bones ached that night
my cheeks were stained from the tears
the pit of my stomach was empty
but heavy
two years of shame, mistrust, neglect
but the day I said goodbye
was the first night I felt ill
I knew I needed to let you go
and it ripped me apart
I remember feeling numb
unable to blink –
as two years of us flashed in my mind
we were always together
yet, I always felt alone
I accepted your flaws
you despised my mistakes
I loved you for who you were
you declined

I healed you

although, I was missing pieces myself

and still felt better

I am one line

you are another

parallel

we will never cross paths again

I guess that is our fate

but I do know

forever by your side I will be

maybe we could

shift realities?

and allow our paths to cross again?

Because the loss of you, will change me forever

I run, and I run

constantly in my mind

back into your arms

though I may be rambling, these words you will never hear

I must say them, or my mind will never clear

what an unshakable feeling

for me to be the pencil markings as I try to write our story

and you, the eraser

I write

you erase

we revise

I wanted more than anything

to give you everything

and I did

brick by brick of myself onto you

but I started to feel bare

as the wind began to blow

shivers and chills up my arms

and down my back

I knew that if we were to crash and burn

You would remain standing

because of the brick foundation I created for you

and I, only ash

you were not protecting me, so

one by one, I started taking my bricks back

and tried building myself up again

but I grew tired

because with every brick I took back

I carried the baggage that came with it

your absence haunts me

late at night, I reach over, and you are not there

I pull the covers close to my face

hoping to catch a glimpse of your smell

but it has faded away

I know I let go

I know I threw in the towel

but it does not change the hurt that I'm experiencing now

I wanted happiness

for you and me

but I did not know it'd hurt this much

I did not know the right thing could feel so wrong

I did not know I was going to feel pain like this

I'm scared to know what moving on feels like

but if I stay and ponder

I'll get dragged like quicksand back into the past

I love you

I miss you

but you deserve better

and I do too

I wanted 100% of you

but I didn't thank you for the days

that you tried your best to be

I'm sorry

please forgive me

this isn't bittersweet

it's bitter

like the tears that are rolling down my cheeks

I'm right here if you need me

but I understand if I only become but a memory

clenched fists

my nails puncturing the skin of my palm

looks like you fell in love again

with someone who isn't me

I knew to never let you complete me

       I did it anyways

I made you my world

now that you're gone – I feel the world on top of me

reminiscing the nights

we spent under white sheets

now under a flickering light

it's just me and my heartbroken poetry

there is a storm on my starry, starry night

my sky dark blue and gray

the clouds come rolling in

dark and heavy

mimicking the darkness that resides inside of me

there is no peace and quiet

my mind screaming to the dark hills beyond

my eyes heavy – ready to water the soil beneath

ready to set the tears free

       I cry with the rain

the drops blend with my tears and cover the ground

it has been 3 months since you've been gone

and I am sitting in a place, we once talked about forever in

I hated those damn cigarettes you used to smoke

now I'm holding one in my hand, contemplating on sparking it

not to smoke it, I never had the desire

but to make our space a little less of me, and a little more of you

the smoke used to cloud our room and we talked for hours

now the smoke arranges into shadows of your figure

I look away and down at the ashtray, the one I bought for you

the ashes are still there – I pour them onto the table

I write the words 'I love you' with the ashes

and my fingers turn black

I hoped you would come down these stairs and see my message in
    the ash

I hoped you would fall to your knees, and tell me you love me too

I take the last cigarette and spark it at last

and memories of you appear in the rising smoke

I miss the times you lit up my life and sparked me with love

you took my breath away, with every look into your eyes

and the seductive look with the inhale of those damn cigarettes I
    despised

the same feeling, I experience now

as I fight back the urge to bring that cigarette to my mouth

I know I'll taste you

but I'm not sure I am prepared

you have stolen my sleep once again

by invading my mind

thoughts of you, thoughts of us

replay over again, on an endless repeating loop

I was okay, I was doing just fine

but all it takes is one word, one song, and one scent

I become instantly triggered

I start to miss you, or maybe I never stopped

It's a different level of pain, missing a lost love

like one by one, stones placed on my back

and I am shoved beneath the ground

I should be sleeping

dreaming of the future and all there is to come

but I am awake, left thinking about you

Place a bookmark to hold your place in the book. This is a lighthouse page. This is your safe haven. Anytime you see a lighthouse icon at the top of your page, it's a sign of safety and provides you an opportunity to check in, to rest, to recalibrate, and breathe.

Take a drink of water! Feel as it nourishes your body. It's important to take time to honor how we are feeling throughout different parts of the day.

Find a comfortable position and when you are ready, start your own body scan. Visualize starting at the top of your head and working your way down to your toes. How does this part of your body feel? Do you notice any pain or tension? Do you feel loved? Happy? Content? Calm? Is your body trying to tell you something? If you noticed any tension in certain parts of your body, just place your hand there and tell that part "I love you." Not only do our actions carry energy, but so do our words. Send love to all parts of your body that need love.

Just take note and keep making your way down.

When you are all complete, continue to drink water and continue reading or rest.

I'm treading deep waters

my head barely above water

heart rate accelerated by the constant kicking of my feet

just to keep my nose from going under

my lungs are working overtime

because my brain acts in scarcity mode

'will this be my last breath?'

then, there are times I'm on the boat

watching the sun glimmer against the water

the waves are gentle and easy

I think about how safe I am and how beautiful the sun is

then my eyes return to the water

and I think about the times, I almost stopped kicking

the times I almost stopped keeping my nose above water

the times I thought 'this is my last breath before I go under'

I long for the times, I get to sail the horizon

and view the sun, watching it rain glitter onto the water surface

I long for the thoughts to go away

I do not want to be reminded of the times I almost gave up

I do not want to be reminded of the times when my world was ending

at any moment, I could begin to drown

soaking my body in herb filled water

the night sky above and I, under the reflection of the moon

the faucet is turned off, but the water continues to rise

I'm beginning to dehydrate as the tears fall down my face

and into the herb filled water

my past creeps in like a robber in the night

longing to steal my heart and break into it

in all the worst ways possible

searching through tear-soaked eyes for something beautiful

my mouth is now covered by the herb filled water

the time is drawing near

I must stop this crying, but I wish you were here

my tears fill the water

and I'm melting into the herbs like candle wax

I weep for the girl in this herb filled water

who just longs for everlasting love

one that reminds her of the cosmic stars that she was created from

for someone to see her heart

and beat along with it, for the rest of their lives

this someone who wants this heart must know it is the strongest

but weakest part of me

for it has been shattered into pieces for years of my life

yet still finds a way to keep beating

I weep in this herb filled water, with hope he sees me and wants me
     still

I get sad because I know energy does not lie

and I know when you shut off

and disconnect from me

that switch in your head

and you keep me at a distance

truth is, I say that I am fine

even when the tears fall down my face

because over the phone, you would never know it

and I'll never admit it

but half of me wants you to notice

to hear that crack in my voice

I'm scared that you won't care

and then I will break even more

I'm running out of pages in my notebook

and they are crinkled, crumbled, and crisp

dried from the fallen tear drops

I just leave them there to dry before closing it for the night

even when we are not together

I can feel your wall

I have no tools, no strength to break it down

when I'm in bed, I dream about your body

how I wish it were holding mine – shaping mine

intertwined and not isolated

truth is, I love you

even when you hurt my soul

even when you create distance

I'm trying my best not to get high

to avoid putting that paper under my tongue

but nothing fills this void

and the absence of you

like getting high

and traveling to another planet

getting so lost in space

downloading light codes and sending them to your heart

I'm trying not to light the green

or pour the liquor – but I am empty

and though temporary

they fill me up while you are away

did it rain on you?

like it did on me?

did the sun hide from you?

like it hid from me?

or....

are you enjoying the run rays?

while I'm here going through change

I am stuck in this puddle

thinking about the times we talked about forever

even if that included bad weather

there is rainfall on my blue skies

the clouds above my head carry time wasted

waiting on you

do you have anything to say?

I thought you and I would make it through the rain

I should have noticed the loneliness I felt when I was beside you, but I was too worried about making sure I wasn't alone. The irony. I felt sad when you missed my biggest moments, but now I'm more disappointed that I didn't celebrate my wins myself. Somehow, from the beginning, we were destined to fall and now I'm asking the universe what lessons I was supposed to learn. I would look into your eyes and wouldn't feel like I was at home. I just wanted someone to come home too, but I was blinded by the truth. Standing next to you in crowded rooms was a new danger. I hated large crowds and you failed to be my security, my peace. I should have felt safe, but I wasn't. Dream state used to be my peaceful state, but next to you my mind is overwhelmed with nightmares. I'd rock myself back to sleep and wait for the sun to rise before I woke. I feared the dark while sleeping next to you. This broken love – the saddest lullaby. I hope I can find the peace that I lost with you, to return to dream state, my peace state.

If the section 'Deep Waters' triggered you in any way, brought up some tough memories, or at times made it hard for you to breathe, please use these affirmations below. They have been typed with love and I hope they reach the pathway to your heart. Read and accept the ones that resonate and leave the rest. Thank you for reading, for being here, for not giving up. Remember, healing is not a destination. Honor the process and journey.

I am okay

I am here, breathing

This moment of my life does not determine who I am

My life has value and meaning

I do my very best, and that is enough

I believe in my ability to get through this tough time

I feel low now, but tomorrow is another day

There is nothing wrong with me because I feel sad

I will honor my body by listening to what it needs

I will honor and accept the parts of me that need love

I invite healing energy into my life

This too shall pass

WADING

I used to visit the beach frequently as a little girl

I'd play a game to see if the waves

from way far back could reach the tip of my toe

I'd move back farther and farther each time

to see if the oceans hugs could wrap me up

and splash me with love

the ocean is different as an adult

lying on the sand, wrapped in a damp towel

feeling the sun on my face

I start to think about lost loves and old friends

I think about the series of events that got me here

-       broken and lost

I no longer used the ocean as a blank canvas to play

I used it to escape my day to day

it was solace

to you:

thank you for sticking around
I know I … I'm not perfect
but you stuck around
that means a lot to me

I'm a poet – a writer
I live in my head
thank you for learning to love me
while I learn to love myself

I look at you and scream internally
"thank you"
no one has ever found me worthy
to stay long enough to…
figure me out
to understand the reasons
and non-reasons
why I live in my head

I'm into music
the lyrics say all the words
to my soul
when my tongue becomes tied
I'll sing to you someday
you seem to naturally,
just bring the tunes

my heart beats to the sound of you

just a glimpse of you
reverses all damage done previously
I'm blessed and honored
to be loving you

I've never been a talker
only these books on my shelves
got me to speak any words
but as the sun orbits around
the stained glass windows
all the colors shape your face
and my vocal cords are smoothed
and tuned
and I want to scream to the world
how you have changed my life

I can be impatient

also, torn between wanting the clock

to go much slower

and if I contradict myself, I'm sorry

but you continue to show up for me

and I start to fall in love with being myself

I caught myself

trapped in my own web of insecurity

I saw you walk towards me

body slender and thin

and I immediately grabbed

the closest blanket to cover myself

the first thing your fingers reach for

and rip right off me

I'm exposed… fully open

in fact, so open

the breeze from the cracked window

blows in and sends chills

down my spine as it touches my skin

you begin to trace the outline of my chin

down my neck

to my shoulders and along my arms

"I'm your safe haven…

you are free to be who you are with me …

I love you for who you are now

and who you aim to be days ahead…

you don't have to hide behind a blanket

or the shadows of your past…"

he spoke to me these beautiful words

as my insecurities crumbled to dust

at my feet

I was born again in love

I am protected

a soft breeze greets my face

I then look up to a bright golden light

suddenly wings appear

I'm okay – I am flying on the wings of my guardians

when I cut the strings that kept us together

I felt such relief

I could breathe again

I felt free

liberated, and I felt gratitude

for I could be myself again

when I cut the strings that kept us together

I felt such sadness

I couldn't breathe

I felt encapsulated

confined, and I felt grief

for I didn't know who I was without you

who knew doing what was right, could feel so wrong?

painting watercolor by the sea

bleeding onto the paper

sea salt wounds from paper cuts

lonely waves, quiet

I could get accustomed to this

the ocean keeps my secrets

oh, how I wish it could speak back to me

here, with the water, my lungs become clear

I feel as if the sea admires my painting

it mimics the pinks and blues

above in the sky

I allow a moment for myself

of stillness and peace

to hear the words from my higher self

she's asking that I lie on the ground

align with my heart center

and allow the ground to hold me

ever so gently

she's asking that I close my eyes

and to see the world

using my other senses

then – open my eyes

to see the clouds above

"take a deep breath" she whispers

"envision the air traveling down to your belly"

in this moment

I allow myself to feel and experience

any emotions that may arise

healing is possible – I am here doing it

I am safe

I deserve to be here

I am my home

attuning to the wisdom of what I already know

I am reborn – to reclaim my lost pieces

downtown coffee shops are my favorite
especially when the rain is falling
there is something about espresso
and watching the raindrops fall down the window

self to self... a self-love mantra

I know you are hurting

and sometimes it is hard to breathe

nights are the worst – when you lose all control

you wonder if anyone is out there

someone who understands

if there is anyone who will listen

you want to know if everything will be alright

but dear self, you are not alone

       I will carry you

I have been here the whole time – holding you

you and I will take over the world

I know you have covered your wings

you are afraid to fly

you wish the weight could be lifted

because the burden on your heart is so heavy

but dear self, you are not alone

       I will carry you

       I will hold you

one step at a time, dear self, you and I

when you come home

and feel like there is no one to love

nor one to love you

       I see that

       it hurts me

because dear self, I love you

       I will carry you

       I will hold you

let those tears fall into my palms

and say you won't let go

even when you feel like you have given up

even when you have fallen

you want to be loved

you long to be needed

well dear self, I need you more than anything

I need you to hold me

say you will carry me

      I love you

Take a deep breath, close your eyes, and give yourself a bear hug. Bring your awareness to how this hug feels. Maybe this is exactly what you needed. Maybe it feels different. Maybe you aren't feeling anything in this moment. All is okay.

If this is an emotional exercise for you, be gentle, be patient, and do this on your own terms. Honor what comes up for you and breathe...

sure, she has a brightness to her

a warm vibrant light and she makes you feel loved

and reminds you that you're not forgotten

sure, she smiles, and the world starts to spin again

       contagious

your frown starts to disappear

but she doesn't show the bad and the ugly – she doesn't show her tears

although bright, warm, and vibrant

she's hidden

amongst her fears and insecurities – she feels forgotten

just when you think you couldn't love her enough – she stays awake

  at night wondering if she is loved

all while –

tapping the wooden surface of the kitchen table

counting the stars out of the window, and wondering if wishes really

  do come true

her father, absent

and her mind wanders

if he couldn't love her

       would anyone else?

he was to be her first love – but he failed her

and all the questions about worthiness flood her atmosphere

she extends her hands to lift you up

always there in times of need

but she lies on the ground of earth

her hands in the air, reaching out for what seems to be nothing

the clouds stoop down and she's fully immersed

she sure is special this girl you see

but it goes much deeper

than what meets the eyes of this brown eyed girl

she writes her feelings onto paper

and in person her words become frozen at the tip of her tongue

yeah, she is warm and vibrant and the light in your darkness

and when she smiles your heart beats a little quicker

but she is reaching out for help

she is reaching for you to be like the clouds

surrounding her, protecting her, loving her

What do you say, if we live out our fate? The one we have created in our minds. If I love you and you love me, for how many years the universe grants us. We can watch the stars that sit up in the sky. Let's jump from planet to planet. Just you and I and watch the dust float before our eyes. What do you say, if we pretend that we are the only ones alive? Then only will it be true freedom. I'll whisper how much you mean to me and you'll shout to the cosmos how much you love me. We will realign our star struck hearts to stay connected forever. You are light and I am light. I do not want to picture my life without you. That's a nightmare I dare not wake up remembering. Stay with me and I will stay with you. Seems like we have spent most of our lives searching for this exact love. Here you are. No substitute, you are the one. I feel like I've been searching for the answer to a question only you could answer. Your love was the answer. You compliment me. What do you say if we grow past the burdens, the ones we carried with us? Let them float away in space and become a meteor. You are the focus magnetized in my personal telescope. With you. The only place I long to be.

the windows to my soul have been opened

the wind from the cosmos flow through my lungs

I've finally found my peace of mind

after spending some time losing it

I put my trust in my guides

in return, they said I'd be just fine

I've learned that even getting caught amongst strong winds

I'm only being taught how to fly

I remember when I was but a small child

sitting in the corner of a dark blank room

   "in my mind"

and tears are rolling down my face

as my index finger kept the shiny globe spinning

I understand now that I was looking at my future

and all the traveling I would do

all the places I would see

and the things I would do

those were not tears of sadness

but instead tears of happiness

as an adult I would find my soul purpose

and live to fulfill it

now I trust the signs – the pictures in the clouds

the dreams I imagine when I close my eyes at night

"I can achieve anything" I say to myself

my message in a bottle – sailing into the ocean

for the universe to receive

It's me, Ana

can you hear me calling?

I'm wading…

the water crashing up on my skin

thank you, Universe, I write in the sand

take my hand and lead the way

I have been sinking in my tears

take my hand and lead the way

I have been crying for far too long

show me the way – the path to happiness

I always take the wrong path

take my hand and lead the way

be near to me, look me in the eyes

do I blend in with the night sky?

because I always felt so invisible

do you really see me?

am I foolish for these thoughts?

when you take me by the hand,

do you see our future?

will you stay close to me?

lead the way – my heart has suffered enough

if you catch my tears – turn them into a waterfall

so that we may dance and purge the sadness away

does time pass slowly when you see my reflection in the water?

do I make you forget time?

take my hand, lead the way

show me love

for I need replenished

the raindrops would fall from the clouds

the faint sound of them hitting the window

was a sign for me to go out and play

I'd tussle in the wind

as it blew my hair across my face

the lightning in the sky

reminded me of my ancestors

the years of lineage

running across the veins of my blood

I wondered if they too played when it stormed

if I got my taste for the dark gray clouds from them

if they collected the droplets in a jar like I do

if they cried with the rain like I do

and just like that, I was one with the sky again

leaving a place that felt familiar

and leaving a person who felt like home

all I could think about was all the non-coincidental occurrences that
   have happened in my life

for the universe to bring me him

I at first wondered why

and questioned why

until I realized the answer that was prevalent all along

to love and be loved

I wanted to take his heart back home with me

I wanted to be thousands of feet in the air, but only if his love would
   be there to accompany me

because flying free, high in the sky

felt nothing like the freedom wings he gave to me

"I love you", I whispered into the infinite air

hoping that even though miles separated us, he would still feel my
   warmth

there is something about saying goodbye

like those final kisses and final words as I parted from you

I have waited so long to feel what I did not know existed

and I look into your eyes to see the cosmos that I was created from

home... I see in your eyes

and until we meet in the skies to reunite

I will hold the universe close to my heart

I will feel you as I close my eyes to sleep

without your flaws, I'm not sure I could love you

quite as much as I do right now

so, the next time you tell me

that your flaws keep you up at night,

I will remind you that they are the very reason why I love you so

I have too many miracles transforming inside of me

I am the sun

but I fear letting you in

because I was the sun before

then I was left, and the light was taken from me

I had to find my light again

but let me tell you, with my open eyes in the dark

      I saw things

I couldn't tell if they were real or just my imagination

but I was scared

so yes, I want to let you in

to share my newfound light

I see you walking in your tunnel

it's dark in there, isn't it?

tell me, you're not here to steal my sun, are you?

if you are here for me, I'll share everything that I have

but promise me you won't leave

I cannot bare the feeling of being cold

and losing the feeling of touch

and warm sun on my skin

I have got bricks at my feet

ready to build a wall, but I don't want to be closed off

but if it means keeping my sun, it's something I'll have to do

but instead, let us take these bricks and build a foundation

so, the sun may kiss me on the eyelids, ready for me to wake

if you take away my sun, I will sleep all night

and sleep the days away too

the sun keeps me from falling into depression

please say you love me for me, and not what I have

they say:

no rain, no flowers

but it has been raining a lot here

too much of anything, can't be a good thing

no rain, no flowers

but there should be balance – or am I being unrealistic?

my flowers are here

and they are growing

but the roots – they are drenched in water

I am like a flower sitting on the windowsill

begging to be grounded and free

so many tears and my shirt is soaked

it is clenched to my skin

oxygen cannot enter

no rain, no flowers

my thoughts whisper hope and optimism, creating dew

I better have a yard full of flowers after all the rain leaves

unravel me

my body covered

I'm on the bed

I know I've been so bundled but my petals are ready to blossom

touch me ever so passionately

ever so gently

ever so softly

unravel me

my body exposed and I am waiting for you

I know I've been hidden but my petals are ready to be seen

touch me ever so lovely

ever so smoothly

ever so calmly

unravel me

my body once burdened, it is ready for love

I know I once was withered but my petals long for a slow watered
   drip

touch me ever so delicately

ever so tenderly

ever so lightly

unravel me

at night, I take all my maps, and edit the ones that lead me away

  from you

death fell in love with life

death had the power to take the life out of anything

flowers, people, animals, trees

people fear death

they run away from it

avoid it

death couldn't understand

and so, death said – "I take away pain, I end suffering"

yet, people still ran away

death envied life, and its ability to touch the ground and watch
    flowers bloom

until one day

death approached a flower

and the flower did not move

it did not run away

unafraid, the flower stood amidst death

and death questioned why

and so, the flower said – "just as beautiful life is, death matches its
    beauty"

because without death, there is no life

the flower knew, that in its place, new beginnings would emerge

a legacy would be born after its death

death began to view life from the eyes of love

people shared their darkest and deepest secrets with death

the reasons why they continue to love life, even with death knocking
    at their door

death loved the power of life, and life loved the power of death

two beautiful counterparts

I wish I could fly to the sky for just one night

I would land on the moon and share my secrets

looking down to see the millions of stars surrounding me

one thing about me, if I say I can fly, I will fly

and so, I wish to jump from planet to planet

sharing my deepest secrets with each one that I land on

traveling the universe, the galaxy at night

now that is a different kind of beautiful

the echoes from the stars reach my ears

Anastasia – resilient, powerful, beautiful, creative

for the stars have always been there, even the nights I felt alone

I can be dramatic, emotional, and overreact

but you protect me

I cry, shut down, and get easily upset

but you protect me

I'm impatient, moody, and live life based off fear

but you protect me

I tell you my secrets and you hold onto them

you grab onto me and love me anyway

you protect me

I like to be invisible, eyes away from attention

you make me the center and then I love it

I crave a solid foundation, a house with loved filled walls

and you protect my wishes and desires

my daddy issues creep up, and I need love more than ever

and you protect me

I carry weight on my shoulders, hold onto past hurt, and ponder
    traumatic events

but you come and offer protection from my thoughts

when I sit in darkness

there you are –

your lighthouse appears to rescue me

you protect me

wildflower

planted, never plucked

beautiful

the wind gently blows her petals open

and his hands begin to vibrate on the love frequency

she's sweet

and the bee's surround her for protection

she makes him dance in tall fields of grass

growing freely and her roots are grounded

she gave him wings to be free too

many have come along, and tried to cut her down

tried to keep her captured and chained to societal expectations

but she planted herself and swore to reject conformity

he loved her for that

she can flourish anywhere

and so, their love did too

she's resilient and beautiful – and he fell in love

she grows in the rain, sunshine

in the wind, and darkness too

she's the flower that grew through the cracks

and he loved her versatility

she filled the world with love – he was included

so, their love story began

let's make a promise to each other | that we won't let our fire burn
out | keep the passion in your heart | and I'll keep the love in
mine | as long as we are together | we will live through the ups
and downs

- pinky promise

you hide yourself from the world, after you believed it robbed you of your magic. little do you know, the stars put on a show for you. you're worth impressing, the moon rises higher in the sky just hoping that you would see. you're worth it. you find the closest rock and hide beneath it, after you believed you were not a masterpiece. little do you know, the sun beams brighter, so that you may feel its warmth, you're worth protecting. you put your heart on a chest full of ice, hoping for it to freeze so that it wouldn't get broken again. little do you know; you're the reason broken pieces became art, and the world would be less without you here. you complete the earth as the earth completes you. uncover yourself and allow yourself to become authentically naked. you hide yourself, but they are looking for you.

Find a comfortable position and when you are ready, start your own body scan. If you noticed any tension in certain parts of your body, just place your hand there and tell that part "I love you."

Just take note and keep making your way down.

When you are all complete, continue to drink water and continue reading or rest.

you show me the moon in the daylight – I show you the stars

we just work like that

sitting in silence and your smile says a million words

you do everything to keep me bright

look at us, we are –

flying, soaring, dreaming, loving

you say the magical words that keep me alive

sitting in silence just you and I

no pressure to be anything

or say anything

just holding space for one another

I accept your truth and love you for who you are

I love you in the silence

that's when your heart speaks the most

and I bring my entire presence to you

I'll walk this journey with you

I'm okay with the destination of your choice

I am here for the rest of time

unconditional love – yes it does exist

it is not I love you, wrote out as a list

and so, I'll tell you what I mean

the nights your hands are crushed to your chest

and sleepless nights when you're unable to rest

anger and fire, the hateful words too

will never be enough, to say I don't love you

the cry out loud and the pain deep within

the days you lose, and the nights you sin

when the tears fall like rain or the clouds turn you blue

it's never enough to stop loving you

if your silence echoes in empty halls

and anger has knocked down all of your walls

the ground collapses or your heart longs to shatter

and nothing at all seems to matter

yes, I still love you

just know that we can never lose when it's just us two

because that's what I mean, when I say I love you

when you don't feel like yourself and the doubt fills your head

you can't get up and you're glued to the bed

when songs and melodies lost their rhythm… the drums their beat

and you're face to face with fear, your hand out to greet

through all of that, I still love you

when the light escapes, so darkness can brew

I'll bring you the light because I love you

take my hand, I will lead you to a place of peace

where you and I will reside, and sleep wrapped in the arms of earth

time escapes our hands, like water making its way through the cracks

tears of happiness flow and we create a river in the peaceful quiet,
    that's surrounded by trees

we build our boat to begin sailing our river – and explore all the
    places love can take us

following the sun – guided by the moon

our destination unknown although the direction is certain as our
    hearts serve as compass

your light guides through darkness

and our freedom, will take us through many lifetimes

the ashes of past lovers are stained on your skin

all their promises to love you and their claims to never leave

unfulfilled love letters running along the streams of your veins

I've been ready to repair, what has been hurt

but know my love, this does not mean you are damaged

I want all of you –

sit here in this warm rose petal bath

while I run my hands down your skin – replacing the stains with my
   love for you

in my arms you are safe – in my arms you are cherished

your love will never be taken for granted

I long to have a drastic change in my life and… I really do believe I am taking the necessary steps to do so. See, I honest to God, believe I will make it to that next level. It has my name written all over it; I am claiming it!

A person like me doesn't struggle for no reason. A person like me doesn't get dragged through the ringer to come out worse. It's not me, and it won't be me.

I, am strong, victorious, and beautiful. Enough is.. enough. It's time to pick up my painted pictures from my head and hang them up on the wall.

My imagination is so creative. I see my life and I paint it. I see what I want, and I paint it. All in my head. I invented this life; I created this world in my head. As God painted me with his creative vision, I came out like this: beautiful. And just like that, I CAN say that everything is okay, things are going well.

Thank you, God, for this life that I live. I make up this co-creation of imagination all in my head. I'd rather be grateful tonight than bitter. I have everything I could have ever asked for. The Universe, God's backyard, blends perfectly in my sky that my eyes project. The sun co-creates with the brown that God painted for my eyes to make Gold – it's visionary, 24 Karat.

Imagine our brains – what we want, we get. We can think of all the things we want to be and see and suddenly, we look to our right and there is another picture hanging on our wall – magical. Isn't it?

Things are going well and sometimes they aren't. It's okay. When things are great, I appreciate the hell out of them. When they aren't, I'm twice as grateful because I know that life is happening FOR me and not TO me. I AM THANKFUL!

I know when I cry – the tears add moisture to the dry ground and it's soft to walk on. For me not to me. I admit that it took me a while to grasp that concept but I'm glad my mind reprogrammed.

God visits me, as I drift. I start to dream. I paint my dreams for him and he paints his equivalent. Wow – they match.. I'm on the right path.

Asleep in a pasture that is covered in green... green grass. Made so well, created so beautifully. It touches your soul at the thought. That grass so soft, you fall asleep. The breeze you feel is God's breath on your skin.

I was falling apart
while falling in love
I'm ready to heal
So I can be better for us both

Say these affirmations quietly within or out loud, whatever is comfort-able for you. You may even write them out into a journal.

I am working towards creating a better life

I no longer place limitations on myself

I am designing a beautiful future

I deserve love and happiness

Bit by bit, I am creating a life that I love

I am growing and learning every day

I am doing my best with what I have

I trust myself enough to learn from any mistake

THE SHORE

Rocking Chairs

I picture us sitting in rocking chairs

under the country stars

with no burden on our hearts

accompanied by the moonlit sunshine

92 and still in love –

sitting in our rocking chairs

reminiscing over our 20's – the nights we spent sitting in a parked
  car

the headlights shining over the driveway

replays of our golden dreams

thinking about our future selves sitting in rocking chairs

talking about our desires of forever

our laugher is treasure tonight under this starry sky

an ounce of silver sparkle from the shooting star

a simple breath of magic

from the words I love you

I hear that if a writer falls in love with you

that you can never die

and this I believe to be true

because I have fallen in love with you

and the scribbled letters and words on my paper

are filled with nothing but you

even strangers in different countries will read my story and be in
   absolute awe

years may pass and days swift by

but my love for you, certainly can never die

pages might turn yellow and the corners tarnished

but in between those many lines – your name will live on

a tale for the generations to come

a love story that has lasted over many lifetimes

my love for you is storybook worthy

and you deserve to live on forever

in my mind, and the millions of readers worldwide

skies change and storms brew

but there is an unwavering love that I have for you

the love that never leaves but builds overtime

I will always be here to catch you

like the catcher of our dreams that hangs above our heads at night

as you journey through life

chasing clouds and surviving storms

I will always hold the precious treasure that resides inside of your
chest

I see you light up in the skies

jumping from star to star

you were born to shine

you are an illuminated love and the lighthouse to my soul

I am in complete awe

you have birthed the brightest of stars and created a path for us to
travel on

I love you

she paints

her brushes scattered throughout the house

canvas hung on cracked walls

she paints a beautiful home for her three children

they run and skip

on creaky wooden floors

they play with sticks and broken army men

she paints flowers for Luna – her baby girl

space shuttles for Roman

and green frogs for Rain

her twin boys

she paints

the house is old, and windows cracked – they share one bed, but
   their life is beautiful

she paints for them, so creativity can brighten their broken home

planting seeds of inspiration

watering roots of imagination

she paints

make me laugh, while I am cooking breakfast in the morning. your hands wrapped around me as I'm stirring the batter in a bright yellow bowl. the sun, shining through the window and the heat I feel on my skin. the birds are chirping outside. "they're happy" I say, while smiling. I laugh because I am too. you take my hand and lead the way. "what about breakfast?" I ask. you lift me gently, and on the kitchen counter I am placed. I never told you that passionate morning kisses were my favorite, but I believe you knew. the taste of coffee lingering, and the strength of your arms pull me closer – I pause and admire the view. not just the blue sky and the white clouds but how the sun shines through the kitchen window and into your eyes. "good morning" I whisper.

you, me, and coffee

when we wake – the sun peaking through the curtains
I look at you and you at me
coffee and sex in the morning
I start the coffee to brew
and walk my way slowly back to you
I climb on top, and watch you rise
the coffee hasn't been consumed – but you're ready to start
you, me, and coffee – I love that I am your remedy
I trace your body with my breath
and your eyes close – like you're falling back asleep
but the brewing coffee aroma slides under the crack of our door
just as you slide into me
you, me, and coffee – add some sex therapy
we go together like cream and sugar – I can't wait
to taste the coffee from your lips
I love our time in the morning
        where you have me for breakfast
you, me, and coffee – I'm your favorite recipe
the hot coffee aroma continues to fill our room

you are my sunlight and laughter
a sweet treat, and dark roast dream
let's go make our coffee
you bring the cream, and I the sugar
as we mix and stir and entwine
        we become one entity

I want you to know that in this moment

coffee in bed is my favorite time of the day

I have been sparked with light – that you have given me

the light of the stars you have given my soul

passing by, people stare

"you're glowing" they say to me

I have been sparked with the light from the universe

and I thank you

oh, how I despised having a broken heart time and time before

but look how easily I am now filled with light

I used to think (my ego)

that I was never good enough – but now I know

I have everything all within me already

you have sparked love within me

you have sparked light within me

all from the eternal source of light and love

because we are connected –

I and universe

you and I

you and universe

so, we became like one

I wake up to rain hitting the roof and clashing into the windows

but there you were sound asleep

I went down the stairs and into the kitchen

to make a thing of tea

my socks up to my knees and a big t-shirt draped above the caps

I open the curtains to watch the raindrops hit the ground

I then feel your arms wrap around my waist

breathing slowly down my neck and −

"hey, you" left your mouth and entered my right ear

I reach my hand up and wrap myself around your neck

you begin humming music so softly and −

my soul is immersed in love

the aroma of cinnamon spice fills the room

these are the nights, moments, and times

that I have framed in my memory

a long hallway full of you and me

picture frames big and small

but each embodying the love we have for one another

I like how you remind me of warm summer nights – how you taste
   like honey

sweet and subtle

you make me free like riding the highway with all windows down

you get the best of me, but know it comes with the worst

but you breathe in the good and let the bad blow away with the wind

together we rewrite the stars – as they help write our story

it is up to you and me, no one can define our destiny

I love how you are my goodnight and I your good morning

you have been on your own for so long – I can show you it doesn't
   have to be that way

let's go admire the city lights and fall in love with the country stars

with your arms that catch me when I'm weightless

you always take me on a new adventure

I find myself lost in the view when you're there across the room

and find my way next to your side like a magnetic pull

your eyes tell me everything that my soul longs to hear

and we have begun to be the keeper of each other's secrets

let's shut off the world and travel to outer space, the stars are waiting it's not so hard to believe – after all

that the same God who made the sun, moon, and creek

also created you and me

he loved us so much

he designed us to meet

I get lost in your kaleidoscope

you constantly fascinate me –

all the different shapes, patterns, and angles

makes you complete

you are full of vibrancy

you say you are broken, but in my eyes – I only see stained glass

all your broken pieces, scattered into a beautiful mosaic

broken and beautiful, look at the masterpiece that you are

your colors blend together, and form a rainbow in my cloudy sky

I breathe you in because you are my breath of fresh air

a beautiful creation – and I get to view you

Grounding:

If you are able, take a step outside barefoot. If you are not able, just visualize this. Both are just as powerful as the other. Imagine golden, deep, strong roots coming out from the soles of your feet and going deep into the ground. Imagine those roots digging deeper and deeper into Mother Earth. As the roots go deeper, so does your state of relaxation. Breathe and tune into your energy and that of the Earth. Make yourself one with this energy. Just being present and breathing. You can spend as much time here as you need. When you are ready, draw back your roots and allow them to be stored safely and secure within until next time.

Continue to drink more water.

next to you, watching the sun rise

and I'm reminded of why I love you

the sun, symbolic of our love

and on our best days, our love shines like the rays

and when the sky gets darker and the storm clouds appear –

we know that just like any storm, it shall pass

and we will watch for our rainbow to appear

with the sun shining right behind us

I am composed of every person who has sparked my life with light

I am thankful for the colorful bits that –

make up all of you

you each make me the person that I am today

and I realize that I am only human but I'm here on this earth to live
   through this experience

my soul recognizes yours, way beyond the physical

and this is how I want to live my life – adding colorful bits to my pallet

that make up all of you

that I become part of you and you a part of me

while we all become a part of each other

creating, mixing, blending

one universal rainbow

thank you to those who never gave up on me

even when my pallet was nothing but black and white

and blended jaded gray

but one by one you all have added light to my story

I will exhaust every resource of my being before I give up on you.

what we have found in each other is rare. we keep each other's

gears in constant motion. so many days lie ahead of us and it's

unsure what they will bring but I do know:

if they bring rain – we have an umbrella

if they bring war – together we are an army

if they bring questions – we have the answers

if they bring wrong turns – we have the map

in any condition and under any circumstance

my piece of our puzzle along with yours will always be

goodnight, I love you

[642]

our love story is published in the cosmos

I will treat you like a bundle of flowers

and hold you ever so delicately

wrapping your insecurities

and dressing them in colorful ribbons

showcasing what you believe to be the worst parts of yourself

to show you they are beautiful

I'd become a florist – and build a grandiose shop

just to show you that all the flowers in the world

could never compare to how beautiful you are to me

I will water you daily and watch the sun glimmer its rays down upon
   you

I want you to grow – and with my love, I know you will

I rise – unapologetically, against the wind that tried to blow me down

against the heavy rain that tried to weigh me down

against everything that came to break me

       I am unforgettable – a force in my own way

I have taken the seeds of heartbreak and planted them

where they now bask in a collection of light

I never stop trying and giving up is not on my path – for I never

   stop reaching for the sun

beauty is my fortress, and my strength is immeasurable

       unwavering light and firm love forever

I stand against all that came to break me

I follow the light and head North to the sun

I collect the beam of golden rays – watching myself become magic

allowing my heart, the freedom to find light, even in the darkest of

   places

emanating the light within to honor my shadow

because I can only truly love when I honor all parts of myself

I have made enough mistakes that filled up my ocean

it took me a while to navigate to shore

the waters were deep, and troublesome at times

which created a tsunami of emotions

      and

it wasn't until much later, did I realize that

      all those times I sank under for a bit

-that

      all those times my feet got tired of kicking

I was that much closer to reaching the shore

it was like I was born again

and on the day of my birth

all the stars in the sky silently exploded

      an array of cosmic fireworks lit up the night sky

therefore, I am proof that miracles exist

we stand together in the water, as

each step we take creates ripples

that vibrate on the love frequency

before you, I was swept off my feet

    by tidal waves

lifted roughly and carried into the deep abyss of ocean

but you gently allow me to be lifted into the calm

and the sand makes its way out

from beneath my toes

mind – body – spirit

3 points – the shape of you (spiritually)

you are what people are attracted to

who you are and the shape of your 3 points

you are whole without having to be complete

you are sacred and special

unique and conscious

your 3 points, mind – body – spirit

are encapsulated by wholeness and oneness

you are eternal and ethereal

your points have never ending expansion

you can reach as far as you desire

as your 3 points work in unison with one another

trust your intuitive brain –

the brain in you that is not limited

learn to own these 3 points as your unique blueprint

your layout – specifically designed for you

one that cannot be duplicated – replicated – copied

it's you

back from the day you were born

it latched onto your being

and birthed the amazing you

that you are today

I am climbing a mountain
overcoming a low vibration
and reaching for the peak
of highest of all vibrations
I am triumphant and eager
I am climbing
I am now flying

your dreams were placed in your being

your mind –

long before the day you were born

you came into this world

with the ultimate knowing that you were here to accomplish them

look at that day –

you remember

just a baby wrapped in a blanket and eyes so soft and gentle

shower that version of you with love

it's never too late to water planted seeds

your truest, purest form of you has never left

it resides deep within your heart space

chase your dreams

today I created a path along the shore
no more knives and needles prodding my soul
but instead,

      air – flowing freely and easily

it was quiet that night

as I kissed your skin – and watched it turn to gold

we dove into the ocean and for once I was not scared

you were my saving grace

the reason I could float on my back –

without fear of going under

your golden skin brightened the dark, deep waters

and led a way for us to swim in limitless passion

thank you for your existence

for coming into my life and changing it

thank you for being the gentle waves

amongst my rowdy sea

watering me and giving me space to bloom

I thought I'd be lost in the current

inflating water wings to help me stay afloat

my sea which was dark and muddy

with you became crystal clear

that night you took me to the sea

you told me to release my fears

and send them along with the waves

I memorized the pattern of your breath

as we sat by the seaside

the water would reach our toes and they sank into the sand

we let our love sing to the pink sky

and the clouds chime a tune

love in the country

tonight – all we have is this dim streetlight

I twirl you around the river rock

cool breezes blow across the landscape

what beauty this country night holds

as the fireflies – flock towards us two lovers

our own personal chandeliers

carved names in the bent but sturdy oak

I hum a melody – your feet follow behind

him to her –

a pretty face and sweet voice
subtle being and soft soul
she flows through me like the wind
her heart holds on
she always fights for our love
standing there looking at her
I question why she chose me
I love to catch her dreams
when she feels lost and scared
I hold onto them – the way she holds onto me
her presence is a graceful blessing
a wisdom keeper,
making her way through the dimensions
a great seeker,
looking for new ways to love me
how could I ever repay her?

Our makeshift home:
I won't forget the times
we ate pizza on the floor
and made pallets in the living room
to watch family movies together
how our visions of owning a couch
was in sight and not far to reach
how the kitchen cabinets
were scratched and in need of TLC
the front door wouldn't close
unless you pressed your body weight
against it — the nights we shivered
as there was no heat in our bedroom
using the heat from one another to stay warm
we searched for the breaker box
it was nowhere to be found
after running space heater to the next
and the lights went out
I won't forget our many firsts
in this makeshift home
like my first excitement to come
home to you after a long day at work
I know the walls were layers deep
with wallpaper and carpet stained
from the previous owners
but this makeshift home gave me
comfort in knowing we would make it
the best with how many ever years

we wanted to give

and when we live in a house we built

from scratch – we will remember our

home that gave us our foundation

Find a comfortable position and when you are ready, start your own body scan. If you noticed any tension in certain parts of your body, just place your hand there and tell that part "I love you."

Just take note and keep making your way down.

When you are all complete, continue to drink water and continue reading or rest.

I asked him what he thought of me:

I think I was expecting something
along the lines of:
      you're beautiful
      you're amazing
      you're kind

but what I got instead touched my soul...

you make the sun on my skin
that much warmer
you make the beauty of the stars
something everyone wants to admire
you make waking up from peaceful dreams
something to look forward to every morning
you are the love letter that mends broken hearts
the reason why bee's move
from flower to flower
you are my favorite love story
and I will recite it as long as I live
a few extra minutes in bed
with you,
is what I looked forward to
the moon rises in the sky
looking for the beauty that you radiate
you bloom where you are planted
I am nourished by your strength

and brilliance

you are unforgettable – so that

even when a thousand light years pass

the light from your soul

will always remain

I just need you

my world is more beautiful

because you are in it

sometimes you catch me staring

every day I find something new

that I love about you

and have memorized even

the slightest wrinkle from joy

I thank you for making room

in your heart, to love me fully

you are, inevitably, pure magic

we started as strangers

you in one state

and I in another

before I knew your name

and fell in love with your face

you were but an imaginary character that –

I drew on my notebook pages

I would read you and know you

… then I'd wait for you

a lost traveler on the sea

I was soaked and falling under

but I kept you above water – the many drawings of you

kept me alive when –

it would have been easier to let go

you kept me from going under

my lifesaver

I will defend your name
despite what they have to say
just like the ocean that
goes on forever
you and I will always be together

I love you

when you are at your best
and when you are barely hanging on

I support you

when you're following your dreams

lift you

when you're falling behind

a million words
barely scratch the surface
of the love I have for you

there is mysterious intelligence in the ocean

where I once was kicking

to stay above the water

where I once begged for change

I sea that it was begging for me

to change the way, I saw my life

life wasn't asking me to tread water

that I could not swim in

it only asked that I dive deeper

&, there I would find my lifeguards

to help me embrace change

deep miracles never came from shallow waters
my time out in the deep end wasn't pleasant
but it brought me here to you
deep miracles never came from shallow waters
from the shore, I can see the waves crashing together
they no longer have the strength to pull me under

I am open to the tides of healing
as I let the water splash upon my toes
my legs, and thighs
I watch as the little droplets trickle down
and back into the sand
every droplet carries my pain away

I AM

I am a breath of fresh air
cold water on a hot day
pollen to the bees
sugar in lemonade
the moon's reflection on the ocean
an astronaut's first look into space
I am what makes life beautiful

what will there be after you?

gray skies and sunken eyes?

wet ground and rain all around?

will I wallow in my sadness?

or grow wild in my madness?

tear-soaked pillows and...

rest, under weeping willows?

there will be trees named after you

flowers that bloom

in the places that you loved

orchestra of birds

chirping to your melody

a smooth ocean breeze

when I whisper your name

I've found a home in many souls

but none like you

the warmth of your flesh

a blanket in the cold

the touch of your hands

makes me feel safe and loved

your soul is the doorway

to my forever home

here would be my permanent address

the place where I will grow

even after all this time?

they ask

especially after all this time

I reply

he has given me

an infinite number of reasons

to continue loving him

he welcomes every part of me

the parts that come

the parts that go

he gently showers with love

the parts of me that I hide

and lifts the veil

between our bodies to connect

and every morning

when we rise

he commits more to loving me

as I do for him

yes, after all this time

water to my body

-      you are

fresh from the springs
crisp, clean, and clear
no longer encapsulated
by the salt of the sea
but, instead
hydrated from the sun charged water
you drench the buds of my tongue
my body fills with light
collecting every moment with you
like the petals that float amongst the water

we will grow every day –
the rest of our lives
is so unknown
and this version of me
might not be for long
the man you are today
will transform over time
we can change together
growing together
watering each other
we still have so much
of our story to write
we won't know
which way the wind will blow
or what the days will show
but we will grow together

when we slip under the sheets

and are surrounded by

each other's warmth

we begin our own adventure

budding and blooming

my world isn't so lonely anymore

he puts in the effort to match me

vibrationally

he is whole

I am whole

and,

together we become one grand

plan in the universe

created in the likeness of the stars

oceans through veins

roots through lungs

air through heart

created in the likeness of the rain

supple juices quenched in the earth

mother Gaia whispers into her ears

divine feminine – they are coming

to witness you

work of art

stroking of the body

sweet pink peonies

plump bum

drenched sheets

curvy waist

infatuating shadow

casted on the wall

delicately painted canvas

unraveled rose petals

coated the floors

a path to their future

love flowing through

the soles of her feet

I am worthy of light
wildly loved
in a world full of infinite possibilities
coming closer and closer
to my truest self each day
filled with my own love and joy
releasing the past
the chains that held me back
to begin following my dreams
passionately
living in the present
finding my way home
allowing myself to feel good
I am worthy of that

I AM –

A driven artist
an enchanting peacekeeper
on a quest of creativity
a quest of true freedom
a sensitive rebellion
- they exist
who sees beauty
in believing in miracles
a mysterious guardian
flowing through change
allowing space for new
& loving every new woman
I grow into

I bless my lover with feminine grace

helping to elevate his soul

the way he as elevated mine

lifting, ever so slighting,

his chin that gravitates towards the ground

igniting him with the flame

from my heart

so, he may rise to his feet

and join me at the throne

his art of loving me

produced fresh flowers

by the gate

he has protected my innocence

I shall protect his strength

Practicing gratitude:

If you are feeling called to write, let's do this! If not, you can say them within or out loud.

Make a list of 10 things you are grateful for. When you are thankful for what you have right now in this moment, you will find how easily it is to run across more opportunities, people, and experiences throughout your life. When you are operating from a place of gratitude, toxic and negative energy has no room to invade your space.

I feel so completely nourished
in your arms that serve as
my roots
I am completely watered
with love – that allows me to grow

once so soft and brittle
I now am deeply supported –
my roots grounded into the earth
our harmonious love story
that which is published
in the cosmos
we are completely aligned
with the constellations
and compatible to one another

currently
I only invite positive
and uplifting vibrations
into my life
I release what no longer serves me
and rinse negativity off into the ocean
where it will sail far away
transforming into waves and creating
something beautiful
I step into safe places only
where I can truly
and authentically
share the truest parts of myself
I honor the parts of me that are
kind, nurturing and sensitive
I am the source of my own intuition
always and indefinitely honoring
all phases of me

the same water I lost myself in

is now the water I'm laced in

delicately

the water drips from his hands

and onto my lips

what a delicious way to poetically

confess the depth of our love

my awakened innocence

stems from the unwavering love

between you and I

for we are far beyond connected

farther than the bottom of the ocean

refusing to get sucked under

again

by the currents

but sucked into a love

so deep

with enough space to come up for air

I am no longer drenched in tears

but soaked by your essence

like a tight wet tee

hugging my body

stretched and liberated –

no longer curled inwards

to hide my beating heart

I AM…

authentically happy

authentically free

& in your arms

I'll forever be

I have learned to embrace
the creative parts of me
and give myself permission
to gently glide along
the lobes of my brain
flowing effortlessly
like a paintbrush on paper
birthing new ideas
and building their home
on canvas
I deserve to enjoy my life
I enjoy creating my world
a mason jar is placed in my heart
and I am free to place
all the love, excitement, and joy
that I desire
for my jar shall overflow
and pour onto you

several years ago

I wrote a poem

and I spoke about the love

I desired

about the love I was

openly inviting into my life

I wanted to find a love so deep

deep as the ocean

to feel the beating of another heart

other than my own

I spoke of how this love

would awaken my soul

enrich my life

and fuel my heart

that even with a frozen earth

my partners love could

burn fire into my soul

our bodies, ignited by the spark

the height of the sun

could never measure

the amount of love between us

I spoke to the universe

it heard me

I now am laced in love

his arms hold me every night

openly inviting my heart

to rest next to his

I found my deep love

his love certainly has awakened my soul

rekindled my burnt out flame

I am brighter than ever

recovery of the heart

listening to your body

honoring the path to healing

taking your time

knowing you are worthy

for

        time, love, space

admitting you deserve

a life filled to the brim

with joy and happiness

and giving yourself

permission to do so

embracing all parts of you

that make up the whole

seeing the bigger picture

you are part of something

much bigger

evolving, transforming, growing

        flowing

go – at your own pace

rest, hydrate, meditate

RISE

if you read my romance poetry –
I'm very much so
admitting that you have access
to the part of my brain
that never sleeps
the part of my brain
where, my thoughts reside
and hold permanent residence
where my favorite love story
goes on for pages
grab your tea
and candied peanuts
you might be here for a while

tonight, I was reminded

by the moon

to let my brightness shine

to,

acknowledge my good qualities

support myself

validate my thoughts

and feelings

wrap my arms around my body

and allow the warmth from my palms

to comfort every inch

love is so universal

that no matter what language

leaves the tongue, or

what words are pronounced

through the cracks and spaces

between the teeth

all understand

on the other side of in love

I watched

as he watched her

his eyes lit with excitement

her smile, innocent, a gentle grin

and I wondered what he thought about

as he stared into her eyes

maybe thoughts of building a home together

3 bedrooms 2 bath 2 children

each holding one in their arms

I wondered if he dreamed of a happily ever after

picturing her dressed in white

walking down an aisle laced with flowers

the way he looked at her

was breathtaking

it was as if, it was just them two

it's me

him watching me

and I watching from the outside in

look at me

drinking my coffee

laughing at his wittiness

touching his kneecap

and placing my head in the space

between the shoulder and neck

I adore this man

he shines light onto me

and gold shines from my skin

into the air

when a woman is loved properly

she glows

and I love watching me be so happy

a golden radiance

kissed by the ocean

roadmap to the cosmos

healing years of ancestral trauma

passing on healthy habits

millions of cells transforming

and rebuilding

holding the future in the palms of my hands

guiding the generations to come

healing the ancestors that came before me

a palace in my heart

thousands of words

love letters

levels of libraries

stored within my soul

a galaxy born

flowing through my blood

have you ever woke up

to the sun in your lover's eyes

a side angle of its rays

unveiling life's hidden secrets

a spark of dew on the tips of their lashes

a golden glimpse of your future together

baby's breath

interlaced within the pupil

morning breeze under warm sheets

have you ever?

love is the air that fills my lungs

love is the ground that connects me to earth

it is the sky

where my angels guide and rest

it is in the stars

that guide me throughout the universe

love is all around

do you feel it?

the trees

the roots connected to the ground

connected to me

to God

the eternal source of love and light

the veins in my body

the strands of my hair

all made from love

the designs over my fingertips

the shape of my nose

the color of my skin

mixed with colors from the galaxy

and the freckles

tiny caramel spots – the stars

love

you see, love is all around

the water...

I am immersed into the undiscoverable

our human eyes have not seen

can you see me?

a second passed and a whisper entered my ear

"welcome... to the Milky sea..."

bioluminescent film coats the top of the water

it's on my skin, filling my pores

in my eyes, they are glowing

I think about how

I've found pieces of myself

everywhere I go

as if I was part of a glacier

many of years ago

I've been scattered

my remains stretch the world

and back again

it explains why I feel myself

in more than one place

dreaming in bed

and in the arms of my love

I've been sparked by the universe

I'm truly loved

to be in so many places

all over the world

I have expressed my desires and intentions

into the open

      into the blackness

into the infinite
I've been touched by the cosmos
luminated by star dust
a blinding light resides within

we are the lovers

those star gazing travelers

counting stars

instead of sheep – to fall asleep

our lungs –

filled with star dust

purified the air with every exhale

look at them, admiring the stars

we are the reason

they shine so bright

Positive self-talk:

This can be different at first if you're not used to such exercises and that's okay. As always, be gentle, be patient, and take your time.

Find a mirror, big or small and with an enthusiastic inner voice, start a monologue of encouraging words. This inner monologue is your hype person who says they are proud of you, happy for you, and in love with you. Positive self-talk can even be the act of refraining from judgment when we make mistakes, like "That's okay, I've learned a valuable lesson for next time." It can be as long as you would like.

the passion and drive of Mars

my ruling planet

I feel deep within my veins

my roots like a tree

I am more than what meets the eye

ruler of Aries, my sign

fire in my soul

a flame that's hard to blow out

I am ruled by the red planet

be fiery be fierce

a flame with an eternal passion and drive

called to action − realigning

called to have courage

to listen to my higher self

I was made from a tiny particle

of hope

      action

           desire

                courage

                     passion

                         love

since the beginning of my creation

when I was but an empty vessel

I have been assigned a plan

to live the best life that I possibly can

I am seeking my destiny

shooting for the sky

landing on stars

more beautiful

than what meets the eye

created to indeed create

surrendering to the flow of love

when I wake at midnight

and roll over to see you sleeping

a million memories play in my mind

you're the sweetest man

and I'm the luckiest girl

I smile as I see your head

gently resting on your pillow

I think about the life

that we will have together

the countless adventures

if we will travel abroad

and it amazes me that

you can do this to me in your sleep

your eyelashes curled so sweetly

lips puckered

with a slight opening in the middle

shallow breathing

I think about how many years we've got

who will get gray hair first

how many kids will bombard our tiny bed

I place my face

in the warmth of your chest

and I feel safe

I know I will be protected for life

and drift back to sleep

it has been so fun and rewarding

getting to discover YOU

sinking into you as I'm drenched with your essence

I fall even deeper in love with you

as each day passes

I looked at my lover outside of the kitchen window

he was mowing the grass, I was sipping my tea

the sun has only been up for an hour

it's the fresh morning sun, you know the kind

where it's low enough in the sky

to peak through the trees

a calm, quiet Saturday morning

I have always longed for a life like this

-simplicity

we hold hands wherever we go

we take pride in that

I love that moment he reaches back for my hand

he is so strong in nature

but his heart space softens as our hands connect

in public or outside

day or night

holding hands for us means we protect one another

that we are a team

side by side

we are unstoppable

when he arrived in my life

I let go of the air in my belly

I stopped holding my breath

he got me to breathe again

I let out the BIGGEST sigh of relief

he rescued me

a tale of two souls

they build castles on the sand

he installed the windows

she the flowers that surrounded

they planted their seeds – together they were home

she glimmers from the inside out

when she speaks of her passions

he finds it beautiful

they become one, not separate like oil and water

but coffee and creamer

mixed to make something even better

they were rich

not in coins or possessions

but in love

at night the moonlight shines on her bare skin

in the morning, the sun shines on his bare skin

he runs his fingers across her shoulders and down her back

so lucky to have this moment with her – he'd never take for granted

thoughts cross his mind like "the universe chose me to love her"

she is magnetic and radiant

he is strong and magnificent

she smiles at the thought of spending forever by his side

the comfort she gave him to be himself

floating on the clouds, they wrote their love story in the air

their souls will live on forever, loving each other – even if the world
    was to end

at night they would dream of the future ahead of them

where they would go, where they would be

knowing that no matter where, love would always remain

they named all the stars – their favorite part of the night

and trying to remember the ones from the night before

she was cloaked in the light of the moon

the stars laced her pure white dress as she wandered into the water

the stars, appreciative of their sight

he gave her wings

she gave him the power to fly

he is her forever

she is his always

his dream come true

her wishes upon a shooting star fulfilled

they were each other's answered prayers

they illuminated each other

created a blueprint of their life together and started to build

he painted her a sunset

she wrote him a moonlit melody

page by page, they combined their stories into one complete book

provided the missing pieces to each other's puzzles

they lived their lives as they were intended to be

an eternal flame placed in each of them

that will blaze brighter, day by day

this is a tale of two souls

who found it in their hearts to meet again on Earth

they made a pact in the realm above

to find each other again, no matter how long it took

to never lose sight of their love for one another

they share their story to all those in love

but to those who are also waiting

when the time is right, they'll be knocking at your door

you won't have to question it; you will just let them in

scripted above our bed on the ceiling

were the lovely words:

"let's grow old together, laughing at our young restless youth"

every day we will begin again, loving like the first time

but more than the day before

getting ready for date night – looking into the mirror

lining the outside of my lips with liner

and putting the finishing touches on my hair

adding earrings, bracelets, and rings

behind me, I see him standing there

the biggest smile on his face

I turn around to ask what he's thinking

but –

"you are my one in a lifetime"

are the words he said to me

-    I manifested this beautiful being

we thrive within one another

radiating at the highest frequency there is

he wants to build a life with me

and make the world a better place

it feels so good

to dance on top of the waters

I once almost drowned in

I tip toe on the tidal waves

and explore the open sea

letting the sea salt splash my skin

allowing the sweet summer sun

to glimmer against the droplets

it feels so good

to dance on top of the waters

I once almost drowned in

his love keeps me afloat
even the weight of the world can't keep me down
I can feel the sun on my skin now
knowing that the stars have aligned
he's always been my way through
especially during times of being lost
he turned my rainy days
into sunny rays
we meet and blend just as beautifully
as the sunset and the horizon of the sea

grow old with me

we can still be young at heart

our gray hair and skin wrinkled

still holding hands waiting for sundaes

you're a warmth I've treasured

and will be grateful for always

grow

through the storms and sunshine

through change and stagnant times

we will grow as we go

our hearts will still beat the same

and when our time is up

I'll see you in the stars

where our love story is a universal best seller

he makes me feel alive

illuminated every time I breathe

he chooses me every day

fully and easily

he loves me from the depth of my soul

to the surface of my being

making love on silky white sheets

flowing fluidly through the milky way

a new planet is created due to our love

we create magic

electrified magic energy when our hands connect

he makes me feel alive

oh! how in awe I am

how the universe created my home in your heart

that I get to fall asleep

to a beautiful starry night

every night…

you are my brightest star

the cosmos live in your eyes

lying my head on your chest

I'm protected with every beat

every beat of your heart

Journal Prompt:

What is the highest expression of who I am as a soul and as a human being?

Remember to drink water as you write as well.

turned my scars into stars

gave them their time to shine

expressive freedom to be comfortable

aligned with the healing frequency

love cured them all

undeniably, soulfully loved

there is magic in a girl like me

one who turns all things beautiful again

he desired me

even at my worst

comforted me with a tear-soaked face

held me when I lost to my insecurities

loved me when I felt unlovable

adored me during my moods

savored me when I would overthink

cared for me when I was numb

protected me from my darkest thoughts

he is loyal

he is true

yes, we are artists

painting each other on blank canvases

passion as the paintbrushes

desire as the watercolor

weaving, drawing, breathing

existing beautifully

sharing our truth with one another

a piece we have created together

a masterpiece for us to always admire

I don't know how many days
I will have of my life
to love you to the fullest
that is why
I will do it every day
holding you so preciously in my arms
loving you fiercely
serenading you passionately
swimming across oceans
fearlessly screaming to the top of my lungs
boldly expressing my hearts burning desires
loudly… every day that I can

I never had to climb the tallest of mountains

nor reach the depths of the ocean

I never had to burn bright like the sun

nor jump a million hurdles

your only request

your only ask of me

was that I be myself

thank you.

I am filled with the eternal healing frequency of love
opened to the highest of heavens
replenishing my lungs with crisp fresh air
touched with empathy and mercy, understanding
blooming in fields and pastures
even the frozen ground beneath my feet
melts into puddles
freeing the tension of the world
mixing desires with answered prayers
petals drape across my skin
weaving the scent of lavender
maybe gardenia
throughout my DNA
dissolving my pain into the running river
I am set free, you see...
this raw, daunting, unfiltered version of myself
is beautiful

it's a beautiful thing to say

that,

in so many ways

we experience God through one another

through our ripples of laughter

and streams of love

through the waves of happiness

and breaths of good morning

we experience God through one another

I have wild dreams

like becoming a best seller

starting a non-profit

changing the world

sprinkling love on every nation

...

he never made me feel like my dreams were too big

instead,

he grabbed a pail

filled it with water

and began to nourish my dreams

the words he spoke were kind

encouraging

and filled with hope

-    this is the man I will marry

I know we are young

and we talk about forever

but what if tomorrow is it?

when the world decides to take one of us

I can only pray that it takes me first

you see, you are much braver,

much stronger, than I

the loss of you will break me

there will be no recovering from that

there would be no living for me

being in a world without you

is an unfathomable thought

our love

strong enough to create tsunami's

that wash away disease

strong enough to create mountains

that put an end to violence

strong enough to create earthquakes

that put an end to famine

strong enough to create hurricanes

that rids poverty forever

strong enough to erupt a volcano

that puts an end to war

this may sound silly

but as I am standing here in this kitchen

preparing our dinner

pot roast, carrots, and potatoes

I sprinkle natures seasoned salt atop

and my heart flutters in my chest

one might ask me, "over seasoned salt?"

and I will grin while staring out the window

feeling that warmth of the sun

braze my skin

I will respond, "no, because of the person whom I am cooking for."

he fills me with so much love
and confidence
there is no room for doubt
or fear
he is that person
the one you tell everyone about
one of the good ones
one of the best ones
the, *how did I exist before you*, ones

I am an artful cosmic being
an embodied woman
existing like waves in the ocean
exquisite, tender, and caring
bathed in sensuality
I was birthed in the stars
cultivating love
and the space for all to be free
helping those to find their way home
wherever home may be for them
the sun in human form
carrying a heart too soft for evil
romanticizing self-love
accepting all the parts and pieces
that make up my whole essence

I won't ever ask you to change
but, if you do, I'll love you still
through all your phases
stages
periods
chapters
& episodes
I love you enough
to never let go
I love you enough
to go with you
but most importantly,
grow with you
through all the phases of your life

koi no yokan

[ko-ee no yo-kan] Japanese

(n). The extraordinary sense upon first meeting someone, that you
   will one day fall in love.

extraordinary it was.

one of the first pictures you sent me

was of where you were

a picture of the sky

how the beautiful sun

lit the sky a dazzling pink

I asked for a sign

with so much certainty that I would receive

"if this person was going to be

someone special in my life…"

I asked to see a heart

I scanned the picture

middle on out

until I hit the bottom left

a group of trees

there was the heart formed from the branches

extraordinary it was.

he reminds me of my favorite book

the one you can't put down

you want to keep reading

getting lost beneath the sheets

constantly curious

ready to leap with my heart forward

flipping page by page

the gateway to our own universe

I have always been a deep feeler

thinker and dreamer

and when he came along

he showed me how deeply I can love too

I hope you never look in the mirror disappointed
you are a work of art on canvas
God took his time on you
your beautiful soul keeps me alive
you are beautifully crafted
it's easy to believe in magic
when I'm looking at you

my love for you

the soil, the stem, the petals

& you,

the bloom

once I began to love myself again

my creativity lit back the flame

in the pit of my stomach

my inspiration flooded my brain

to find the words that would fill my future book

my visions flashed over my eyes &

suddenly the world was no longer

a dark, dim, black and white

my life began to exist –

as beautifully as spoken poetry

and slow autumn tunes

playing behind orange and yellow leaves

the devotion I had towards my healing

meant I could see glitter again

that all the dullness I created

was becoming shiny again

how I could call on my heart

and it was no longer afraid to answer

when I speak from my heart space

he hears my desires

my wants and wishes

I express my needs loudly

-    passionately

and he never misses a beat

I let him know what helps me feel safe

and like a weighed blanket

he provides that calmness to my soul

we are deeply connected

my atoms to his atoms

he becomes activated by my divine feminine

when I feel seen by him

fully seen, and accepted

... I rise

he never takes me away from myself

fully encourages me to never let go

of that beautiful image I have of me

that he loves her, accepts her

and is willing to flow with the ever-changing parts of her

my softness is embraced by his hands

weaving a path to my heart

a gentle cloud to travel

I invite you to take some time for yourself to invite love into your space.

I am blessed, loved, and supported.
I deserve to be happy.
I accept all of me with love.
I am beautifully unique.
I love who I am.
I am a gift to the world.
My body is a gift.
I am enough.
I deserve to be whole.

My wish for you, is that you know you are so loved and supported. You deserve all the love in the world. You deserve to be here, and I am so glad that you are.

Anastasia

I understand that he has internal battles

things that are hard to speak about

words caught upon the tongue

trapped and stuck to the tastebuds

screaming but others around hear whispers

... I want him to know that I hear him

I support him

showing him that he's good enough

he is committed to healing

and breaking generational curses

reprogramming his DNA

while becoming a better man

for himself and family

working closely with his emotions

and speaking his truth

rejecting everything that keeps him from his soul self

bearing his greatness in this world

for the greatest and highest good of all

home in my heart

when your hand reaches for mine

growing old with you

will be my favorite story to tell

I am ready for the wrinkles around my mouth

the lines below the chin

the creases at the corner of my eyes

I encourage their presence

the fabric of my youthful soul

is woven into my smile

you bring that out of me

I smile more because of you

where none other have traveled

you eagerly await

there is a place for you

in my cingulate cortex

forever...

my favorite time with him
out of many, it's hard to choose
is our space in the shower
completely open
and rinsed from the day
we allow our bad days
our worst moments
the challenges that we endured
to spiral down the drain
it's no longer ours to carry

in doing so
we open our hearts to one another
intimacy at its greatest high
magnetized by the depths of our souls
it is in our silence that he can hear my heart
the way it beats for him
in all the ways it bleeds for him
even the silence of the drops
falling onto the skin
rhythmically dance to its tune

I used to feel

the deep burdens of my sensitivity

feeling crushed by sadness

carrying guilt that was not mine

pressured to force happiness

caved in by the world...

but fiercely I have risen

as a sensual embodied woman

vast and rich in colors

exquisite by nature

I now have an enormous light

that beams from my crown

and drips onto my heart

cultivating love, blossoming my auric field

my emotions have watered me

nourished my body and soul

I remember my sensitivity

as a gift from God

instilled while in the womb

I have a deeper understanding of my place in this world

now, more than ever

I feel deeply called to shine my light

in all ways possible

being my own alarm clock

rolling out of bed on my own time

sipping crisp water

opening the curtains

inviting the sun into my home

sitting on the floor, allowing the rays to fill my cup

mantras, affirmations, meditation

gratitude for the present moment

ready to offer my services to those longing for healing

reading poetry, sipping black tea

painting murals, eating fresh fruit

cultivating acres of garden, making spicy salsa from homegrown
    tomatoes

healing, growing, learning

loving who I am now, forgiving who I once was, and building the
    woman I will be

I am happy to be here

full of divine magic

alluring

magnetic

free

....

that is how I feel when he is around

I feel so sacred in his arms

he takes my fears

& turns them into love

it feels so good to be fully witnessed

my eternal being accepted

satisfying the thirst that my soul craves

my feminine senses are awakened by his touch

his sensual soft masculine

provides comfort and ease to my presence

I'm allowed to bask in my essence as a woman

unafraid and unfiltered

he holds space

cradles me from evil

creating room for me to delve into my playful nature

he's gentle enough

not to wilt my blooming rose

but fierce enough

to capture my soul and send me rushing into mountains of love

today, and every day forward
I am committed to my healing
calming my nervous system
soothing my fears
releasing toxins
alleviating the tension that I carry
softening my reactions
holding my emotions
I deserve to live a life that I love
free from pain, anxiety, and fear

now I rest my head to sleep

anticipating the morning

when I get to witness the sun

greet your eyes

the birds hum your sweet melodic name

my lips but a breath away from your ear

whispering good morning

I carry a special place for you

in this beating heart of mine

here in this bed

watching the sun

glimmer gold specs into your eyes

the only place I want to be

I want to share my life with you

painting a beautiful life for us

one that gives me more mornings like this

he loves every version of me there is

the woman I was yesterday

the woman I am today

the woman I will be tomorrow

as I evolve and grow

he's there

getting to know me all over again

he's committed to learning about me

I used to hate the pain

every ounce of it

questioned it

analyzed it

asked why it was happening to me

until I realized

it all happened for me

it gave me a reason to write

my name is protected

in rooms where my presence is absent

he wears my name on his lips

defending its honor

& all who speak evil

or wrong behind my back

will be shot down energetically

he protects me

she who loves herself unconditionally

lives wildly and unapologetically

I am free – for the first time in years

I can breathe

being seen, felt, heard, and touched

on all the parts of myself

I once used to hide

to be honest,

I always held an amount of doubt in my heart

that I wasn't truly capable of receiving

the deepest love that the world had to offer

to love and be loved

to feel the love deep in the core

that's rare,

but it's real

being seen and embraced

for your true self, your raw self

it's divine

and I have it now

I craved another soul whose existence alone could swoon me and,

cradle my heart gently while taking me on the wildest journey of my

  life

and he does it so perfectly

just when I think it cannot go deeper

I am reminded that his well of love for me

is eternal

it has no ending

I have always wanted to be loved like that

he truly is the soul of my dreams

my capacity to receive his love

is as vast as the universe

always growing, always expanding

I can breathe again

the best part is

I did not have to be completely healed

to be any more deserving of his love

he was there

with open hands, open arms

I could live in this moment forever
when you walk through the door
after a long day of work
dirty from head to toe
your warm arms wrap around my body
I could live in this moment forever
being enclosed in your arms
I feel like sacred treasure

union is the goal
the destination
and we are on the way

I am heaven sent
& in his presence I never feel less than
I am from a place
where souls are dipped
laced
and covered in unconditional love
& in his presence I never feel less than
my flame is never dimmed
only ignited
& together,
we can keep warm, all of existence

there is a poet in the sky

that sends words down to me

I hear the whisper in the mind

and see markings on the tree

there is a poet in the sky

that assists me while I write

maybe it's my higher self

or the angels that protect at night

all I know, that in my mind

are all the poems I long to find

as a gift from heaven

to bring to Earth

my eternal being is magic

becoming in touch with my body

will always be my greatest achievement

I thrive when I'm in touch

I evolve when I'm aligned

I transform when I'm balanced

SAND CASTLES

his hands passionately hold me
the love is spilling from his heart
and all over me
the heat boiled between us
the sweet condensation of sweat
dripping down from our necks
he lures me in
with talks of holding space
creating a place
where I can get completely naked
my soul fully exposed
making sure I'm fully seen
fully heard

my crazy has never been shunned

in fact, he says, I have been mislabeled

my "crazy" as he says

is a woman who cares

he loves me wildly and freely

he holds no resistance to my curiosity

as my mind is free to roam and go as it pleases

cosmic bliss is created when

our bodies taste and nurture one another

we are harmonious

the entire universe I can taste on my tongue

when we breathe into one another

it is in the moment that I feel protected

when I can let my wild side appear

my grip on control is released

& the pressure is no more

I am a wild, wild woman

messy, loud, yet creative

it is two a.m.

your eyes are glistening

resembling the moon light

kissing the water

I'm a good woman

but a bad girl

my pleasure is my power

& I can see the thirst on your lips

fill me up while I fuel you

together we create magic

igniting realms of beauty

that surrounds us tonight

& when you're tuned in

baby that's when I'm turned on

we don't call it sex

we call it soul searching

for when my wrists are bound

and my body is pinned

I am tapped into my sensuality

& all of my splendor

we don't call it sex

we call it art making

for when his fingers run along my body

and my body is his canvas

I am tapped into my creativity

sweet, sweet, love making
while listening to the crashing of the waves
as you crash into me
exploring one another
like a wonderer on the seas
every cell in my body dancing with pleasure

we both bring love to the table

feeding ourselves a spoonful of each other's love

filling up on each other's wholeness

saving room for dessert

our magic tastes so good

I am a magnetic woman

my feminine

my divine

my eternalness

it's authentic

I am my most valuable resource

I long for my partner in so many ways

it does not have to be explained

nor described to anyone else

my desire to witness my partner

in his divine masculine

opens me deep into my core

making love to one another

a different way

every day

the touching of our bodies

the gazing into the eyes

caressing each other's wounds

tenderly kissing of the forehead

how we carry each other's voices so lovingly

hugging each other tightly

laughing together with tears of joy

that's the beautiful thing about love making

it can be a million things

tonight, we venture into each other's unknown

I wildly crave to be plucked

to fully be reached as the priestess that I am

while you…

wildly crave to create a pathway

for my heart to travel towards yours

& your wild imagination to orbit my womb

& my fiercely creative mind to solve your mystery

My laugh, with you, sounds so happy
it comes from deep within
I love the sound of my bellows
as the vibrations tickle my throat

can you hear it?

the beating of my heart

can you see it?

the wind blowing through the front window

catching glimpse of my dark brown eyes

as the sun peeks through the leaves on the trees

can you feel it?

the emotion as I burst with joy

while roaring out loud full of life

I can... to it all

I wake each day

choosing to hear, to see, to feel

fully inspired by all that is around me

the beating of my heart

the wind blowing through the window

admiring my dark brown eyes

fully and expressively bursting with joy

roaring full of life

my life is marvelous

my life plot is interstellar

Sending a huge THANK YOU out into the world. Thank you for taking the time to read my book, to see my thoughts on paper, and for being here. I may not know you, but I am happy you are here.

I hope my words were there for you during your times of need, sorrow, & love.

I would love to hear from you:

anastasialindsey@anampoetry.com

Instagram: anamariepoetry

Website: summersolacehealing.com

About Atmosphere Press

Atmosphere Press is an independent, full-service publisher for excellent books in all genres and for all audiences. Learn more about what we do at atmospherepress.com.

We encourage you to check out some of Atmosphere's latest releases, which are available at Amazon.com and via order from your local bookstore:

Until the Kingdom Comes, poetry by Jeanne Lutz

Warcrimes, poetry by GOODW.Y.N

The Freedom of Lavenders, poetry by August Reynolds

Convalesce, poetry by Enne Zale

Poems for the Bee Charmer (And Other Familiar Ghosts), poetry by Jordan Lentz

Serial Love: When Happily Ever After... Isn't, poetry by Kathy Kay

Flowers That Die, poetry by Gideon Halpin

Through The Soul Into Life, poetry by Shoushan B

Embrace The Passion In A Lover's Dream, poetry by Paul Turay

Reflections in the Time of Trumpius Maximus, poetry by Mark Fishbein

Drifters, poetry by Stuart Silverman

As a Patient Thinks about the Desert, poetry by Rick Anthony Furtak

Winter Solstice, poetry by Diana Howard

Blindfolds, Bruises, and Break-Ups, poetry by Jen Schneider

Songs of Snow and Silence, poetry by Jen Emery

INHABITANT, poetry by Charles Crittenden

Godless Grace, poetry by Michael Terence O'Brien

March of the Mindless, poetry by Thomas Walrod

In the Village That Is Not Burning Down, poetry by Travis Nathan Brown

Mud Ajar, poetry by Hiram Larew

To Let Myself Go, poetry by Kimberly Olivera Lainez

I Am Not Young And I Will Die With This Car In My Garage, poetry by Blake Rong

Saints of Sacred Madness, poetry by Joyce Kessel

About the Author

ANASTASIA LINDSEY is a timeless soul and author who participates in inter-dimensional traveling and building beautiful poems to capture the hearts of souls around the world in the most loving and supportive ways possible.

This humble writer was born and raised in a small town in Illinois where she currently resides in a beautiful, cozy little house on a patch of land with the love of her life, Dakota.

Anastasia has been writing since grade school and has always used empathy, pain, and—most importantly—love as her muse to write poems that help heal. Although an author, she is also the owner of a small business, Summer Solace Holistic Healing & Poetry, where she uses different modalities to help others heal, including Reiki, Meditation, Sound Healing, Hypnosis, and has recently started her journey into Shamanism. Just when others think there couldn't possibly be more, she always enjoys painting, drawing, crafting, and singing. She even auditioned for *The Voice* in 2017.

Her angelic soul and empathetic nature make her one of a kind in this world. Her words take you on many journeys with the strong hope of allowing you to return back home, safe and in love.